Easy E-Book Publishing

H. L. Fourie

Copyright © 2014 by HL Fourie

Table of Contents

Table of Figures

Introduction

E-Book Publishing is a growing market and it is now reported that the sales of E-Books on Amazon have exceeded that of printed books. If you want to write an E-Book and self-publish it, now is the time to do just that. There are several on-line book publishers like Amazon and Barnes & Noble that will let you self-publish your own E-Book for their reader devices the Kindle and the Nook.

First you need to do some research to discover what you audience wants and match that to your passions and interests. If fiction is your forte, you need to choose a genre such as children's books or fantasy. For non-fiction there are a multitude of niche topics for which you can write a book that addresses the need for information on a specialized area. To do this market research, go to Amazon.com and browse through their bookstore. Find the 10 best-selling books on the genre in which that you are interested and examine the table of contents for these books.

From this research you should be able to determine the length of the books, popular topics and themes, their writing style and the target audience. This will provide you with the background information to guide you in selecting a topic for your own E-Book.

Answer the question as to what your motivation is for writing the book, why is it important for you to share your story with your readers. Maybe you have had a unique experience, or have specialized knowledge that others would find useful. It may stem from your own hobbies or interests. If you are passionate about something you will find it easy to translate that into a book.

Write down your ideas and thoughts about your E-Book, just scribble your thoughts into a notepad. Carry a tape recorder and capture your thoughts whenever something relevant comes to mind. As you proceed you can assemble your ideas and plan a rough overview for your E-Book.

Once you have a good idea for your E-Book, start with a rough outline of chapters and then start to work consistently. Treat this as a serious project. Successful writers are those that work consistently and don't give up.

This book introduces you to the steps to easily publish your E-Book for the Kindle and the Nook. The steps are fairly straightforward if you have the right tools. These tools can be downloaded from the Internet. I will give the URL information to do this.

There several ways you can do this and it depends on the tools you have available. I will recommend the best tools you can use to create your E-Book in the shortest time. There are several steps involved in creating your E-Book.

- First, create the content for your E-Book content. For a novel that will be text, but for some books there may also be images and tables.
- Next you need to translate from your E-Book's source format to that used by the E-Book reader device. The two popular E-Book reader devices, the Kindle and the Nook, each have different formats. The Kindle uses a proprietary MOBI format and the Nook uses the EPUB format.
- Then you need to verify that your E-Book appears on the reader device as you would expect it.
- Finally you need to upload your E-Book to the publisher's web site. This will involve registering an account with the E-Book publisher, either Amazon or Barnes & Noble.

This book will help you by walking you through each step you need to take to format the content of your E-Book for Kindle or the Nook. You will learn the minimal amount about HTML and

GIMP needed to get you to self-publish your E-Book as fast as possible so you can focus on the content of your E-Book.

This book is divided into several chapters, organized by subject.

Chapter 1: E-Book Publishing

This chapter provides a description of the E-Book publishing. It covers the different E-Book formats as well as the structure of E-Books.

Chapter 2: HTML and CSS

This chapter introduces HTML and CSS and discusses how to use the elements of HTML and CSS to write your E-Book.

Chapter 3: Organizing the Contents

This chapter goes into how you can arrange the contents of your E-Book document using HTML files.

Chapter 4: Images

This chapter describes how you would include images in your HTML document. It also describes how to capture and edit images.

Chapter 5: Publishing for the Kindle

This chapter describes how to publish for the Kindle. It describes the E-Book formats and tools required to create Kindle E-Books.

Chapter 6: Mobipocket Creator

This chapter describes the Mobipocket Creator that is used to generate the MOBI E-Book files needed for the Kindle.

Chapter 7: Publishing for the Nook

This chapter describes how to publish for the Nook. It describes the E-Book formats and tools required to create Nook E-Books.

Chapter 8: Sigil

This chapter describes the Sigil program that is used to generate the EPUB E-Book files needed for the Nook.

Chapter 9: Calibre

This chapter describes the Calibre program that is used to manage and E-Book library, convert various E-Book files formats and generate files needed for the Nook and Kindle.

Chapter 10: Further Reading

This chapter lists reading resources that provide more background and detail on HTML and E-Book publishing. It includes websites where the tools and programs mentioned in this book can be obtained.

Glossary

1 E-Book Publishing

E-Books are the new media for publishing in the 21st century. Amazon and Barnes & Noble have been selling their E-Book reading devices, namely the Kindle and the Nook, to the growing audience of readers. In fact in 2013 the sales of E-Books exceeded that of printed books. They also offer the ability for anyone to write an E-Book and publish it using their E-Book publishing services.

Their E-Book publishing services let you upload your E-Book to their system and then offer your E-Book for sale on their E-Bookshop.

If your manuscript is a Word document you may encounter problems with the conversion to the formats required by E-Book readers because Word adds additional code that makes editing the HTML more difficult. For this reason I recommend that you simply write your manuscript directly in HTML.

E-Book Structure

E-Books have a well-defined structure. An E-Book consists of one for more HTML documents wrapped in an envelope that is understood by the E-Book reader devices. The wrapper also includes metadata information about the author, the date of publication and the table of contents. Figure 1 shows several HTML documents (each of which may be a chapter in your book) in an enclosing wrapper.

E-Book Wrapper

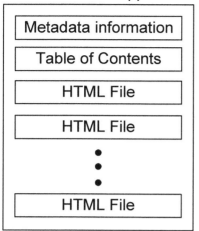

Figure 1 E-Book structure

Formatting HTML Content

An E-Book is essentially a set of HTML formatted documents. An E-Book reader device presents the content of each HTML document in the E-Book in the same manner that a web browser, like Internet Explorer, or Firefox, displays the content of an HTML-formatted web page.

An E-Book does not have a fixed page oriented layout, but instead, it is essentially a re-flowable HTML document whose presentation on the actual reader device depends on the size and orientation of the reader device, as well as the type and size of font selected by the reader. E-Book reader devices are essentially HTML browsers which allow the re-flowable display of the E-Book's content.

Re-flowable means that, rather than each page being displayed in a fixed layout, the layout of the pages of an E-Book depends on several factors such as the dimensions of the reading pane of the reader device, its orientation, either portrait or landscape, and also the type and size of the text font.

Since the E-Book reader devices actually present the E-Book using the HTML information I recommend that you use HTML as your source format. Using HTML as the source format will give you the most control in being able to format your E-Book as you desire. The HTML document can be converted to correctly formatted files used by the Kindle and Nook.

You will need to know a little bit about HTML tags. I will provide some HTML tag templates that will aid you in creating the HTML files. There are also many tutorials on HTML that will help you understand HTML syntax.

You will need three types of tools for publishing you E-Book.

- Text Editor. This will allow you to edit your HTML file.

- Convertor Tool. This allows you to convert the HTML file to the E-Book format required by the E-Book publisher.
- E-Book reader device or emulator program. This is used to verify the appearance of your E-Book.

Firstly you will need a text editor for your HTML document. This will allow you to edit the content and the HTML tags to achieve the presentation that you want for your book.

You will need a tool that will convert the HTML-formatted book into the format needed by the E-Book reader device. Kindle uses a proprietary format called the MOBI format and the Nook uses the EPUB format. You will need two different tools to deal with the conversion for HTML to the right E-Book format. Kindle recommends that you use the Mobipocket Creator to import HTML files and create a Kindle E-Book.

There are also tools available for converting HTML formatted content to EPUB formatted E-Books. You can use Calibre or Sigil to edit your HTML content and to convert them to an EPUB document.

You will also need load your E-Book onto an E-Book reader device and verify that your E-Book appears on the reader device in a satisfactory manner. If you don't possess such a reader device then a software reader program that emulates an actual reader device can be used. For the Kindle, Amazon recommends the Kindle Previewer. The Kindle Previewer lets you open your E-Book and page through it. It allows you to select different devices to emulate, e.g., Kindle Fire, Kindle for iPad, change the orientation and font size, and also test your table of contents. The Nook has the Nook for PC program that you can use.

These programs will be discussed in detail in later chapters.

2 HTML and CSS

Before we discuss the specifics of publishing for the Kindle and Nook reader devices we want to give a quick overview of Hypertext Markup Language (HTML) and Cascading Style Sheets (CSS). Although there are many HTML tags we will focus on a small sub-set of HTML tags and CSS properties that are most useful in creating an E-Book.

HTML defines a set of tags that are used by the HTML browser, or the E-Book reader device to control the formatting and presentation of the actual content. Tags are instructions enclosed in angle brackets, for example **<p>** and **</p>**, that direct the browser or E-Book reader on how to display the content of a web page or an E-Book.

CSS operates in conjunction with HTML tags to provide a consistent appearance for a set of tags.

Editing the HTML Document

Before we go further you need to learn how to edit an HTML document and then see what it looks like from a HTML browser. To edit a HTML document you need to use a text editor which is different from a word processor such a Microsoft Word.

There are several HTML editors available. One approach is to buy an HTML editor that allows you to view both the HTML language and the document as it would appear in a HTML browser. Alternatively, for those on a budget you can use jEdit or TextPad to edit your HTML document and use a browser to view the HTML result. We will briefly introduce you to jEdit and TextPad in the next sections.

jEdit

jEdit is a free text editor and can be downloaded at `http://www.jedit.com`. Download and install jEdit, then start the program to see the initial screen shown below. To create a new HTML document click on **File > New**.

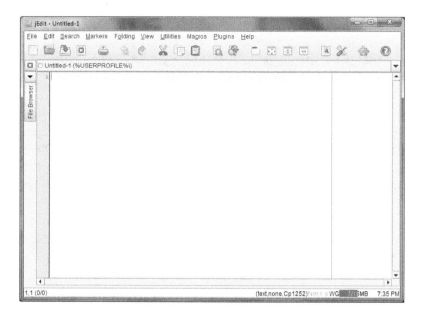

Figure 2 jEdit

Enter the HTML that will be described later in the E-Book. Then click on **File > Save As...** to save it as a new HTML document.

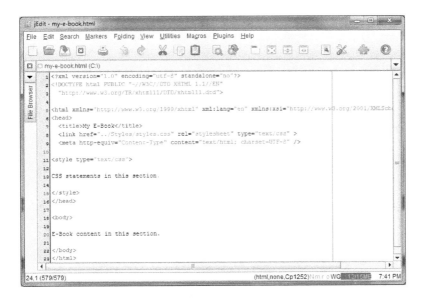

Figure 3 jEdit with HTML document

TextPad

TextPad is a free text editor and can be downloaded at http://www.textpad.com. Install TextPad and start the program to see the initial screen shown below. To edit a new HTML document click on **File > New**.

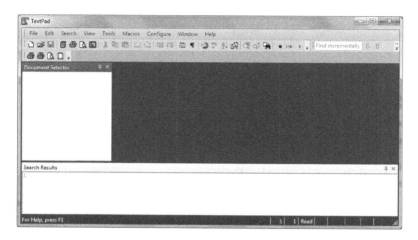

Figure 4 TextPad

Enter the HTML that will be described later in the E-Book. Then click on **File > Save As...** to save it as a new HTML document.

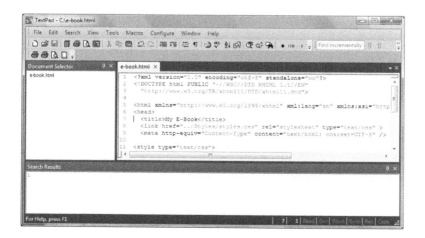

Figure 5 TextPad with HTML document

HTML

An HTML document consists of the actual content to be displayed as well as a set of tags (instructions used by the document viewer or browser to control the appearance of the text). These tags include links to other points in the same document, headings, text formatting like underline, bold, italic, etc.

In a well-formatted HTML document most tags, e.g., **<p>** should have a corresponding end tag **</p>**. Some tags have one or more attributes that are part of the start tag itself. For example, the image **<img>** tag has a **src** attribute with a value that is name of the image file to be used:

```
<img src="images/my-image.jpg"/>
```

A brief summary of important tags is given below.

- Document formatting tags
- Paragraph tag
- Heading tags
- Text formatting tags
- List tags
- Anchor tag
- Image tag
- Tables

A complete description of HTML tags can be found here.

```
http://www.w3schools.com/html/
```

Viewing the HTML Document

To view the HTML file simply use your browser to open the HTML document on your computer. On older versions of Internet Explorer or Firefox, just go to the 'File' menu, then select '**Open**' or '**Open File**' to open the HTML file on your computer.

On newer versions of Internet Explorer that menu is not present, so you need to open files by pressing the **CTRL+O** keys, which will display the 'Open' dialog shown below.

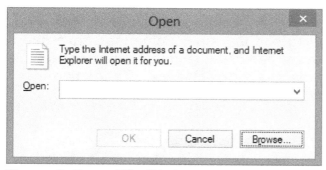

Figure 6 Open File Dialog

Open an HTML file with the text editor and try this as you read through the following sections. As you make changes to the HTML file with the text editor and save it, you must click on the 'reload' icon to make those changes visible in the browser.

Initially all you will see is an empty page.

Document Formatting Tags

Document formatting tags are used to organize an HTML document.

1. **<html>** tag. The start **<html>** tag and the end **</html>** tag enclose the whole HTML file.
2. **<head>** tag. The head section includes title information and various HTML directives. The start **<head>** tag and the end **</head>** tag delimit this section.
3. **<style>** tag. The style section is part of the head section and contains CSS style definitions. The start **<style>** tag and the end **</style>** tag delimit this section.
4. **<body>** tag. The body section contains the actual content of the document. The start **<body>** tag and the end **</body>** tag delimit this section.

An HTML document is arranged in the following major sections:

- the head section,
- the style section
- body section

The complete HTML document is shown below. The text shown in bold is the only part of the document you need to modify. The rest is boilerplate that is required by all HTML files.

```
<?xml version="1.0" encoding="utf-8" standalone="no"?>
<!DOCTYPE html PUBLIC "-//W3C//DTD XHTML 1.1//EN"
  "http://www.w3.org/TR/xhtml11/DTD/xhtml11.dtd">

<html xmlns="http://www.w3.org/1999/xhtml" xml:lang="en"
xmlns:xsi="http://www.w3.org/2001/XMLSchema-instance">
<head>
 <title>My E-Book</title>
 <link href="../Styles/styles.css" rel="stylesheet"
type="text/css" >
 <meta http-equiv="Content-Type" content="text/html; charset=UTF-
8" />

<style type="text/css">
```

CSS statements in this section.

```
</style>
</head>

<body>
```

E-Book content in this section.

```
</body>
</html>
```

Figure 7 E-Book HTML File

Paragraph Tag

The paragraph **<p>** tag is used to delimit text into paragraphs. The **<p>** tag starts a paragraph and the **</p>** tag ends the paragraph.

Heading Tags

Heading tags **<h1>**, **<h2>**, etc. are used define the chapter and section headings. The heading text is enclosed between a start heading tag **<h1>** and an end heading tag **</h1>** as shown below.

```
<h1>Chapter 2</h1>
```

Headings are important as they will be used by various tools to create the Table of Contents. Typically a novel will only have one level of headings, e.g., **<h1>**, for each chapter but some books may have several levels to delimit sections and sub-sections.

Text Formatting Tags

These tags are typically used to format individual words or small fragments of text within a paragraph. Text formatting tags include **<big>**, **<small>, <bold>**, italic **<i>**, underline **<u>**, strikethrough **<s>**. Start and end tags delimit the affected piece of text. For example, 'The **quick** *brown* fox <u>jumped</u> over the lazy dog.' can be formatted like this:

```
<p>The <bold>quick</bold> <i>brown</i> fox
<u>jumped</u> over the lazy dog.</p>
```

Image Tag

Images files can be placed into an HTML document using the **<img>** tag. The **'src'** attribute specifies the URL of the graphics source file.

The **'height'** and **'width'** attributes should be set to the pixel dimensions of your image. For example, to include the JPEG image file my-image.jpg in the sub-folder 'images' use the **<img>** tag shown below.

```
<img border=0 width=449 height=480 src="images/my-
image.jpg">
```

The **'align'** attribute lets you align the image on the left or right of the screen.

```
<img src="buffalo.jpg" align="right">
```

Other attributes are:

- **border** - sets the border width around the image

- **hspace** - sets the horizontal spacing between the image and the text
- **vspace** - sets the vertical spacing between the image and the text

```
<img src="buffalo.jpg" border"2" hspace="10"
vspace="10">
```

List Tags

Lists are used in many documents to present information in an easy to understand manner. HTML lets you create several kinds of lists:

- ordered lists
- unordered lists.
- definition lists

Ordered lists

Ordered lists are those where is items are presented in order: either numerical order or alphabetical order. For example here is an ordered list:

Top 2002 Boston Marathon Finishers

1. Rodgers Rop (Kenya)
2. Chris Cheboiboch (Kenya)
3. Fred Kiprop (Kenya)

Unordered lists

Unordered lists are those where is items are not in any order. For example here is an unordered list:

Shopping List

- Chocolate Fudge ice cream
- Oreo cookies
- Butterfingers

Definition lists

A definition list is what appears in a glossary where you can define various terms that you use in your document. For example here is a definition list:

HTML Definitions

HTML
    HTML stands for HyperText Markup Language
Element
    An element is made up of two tags and the content between them.
Attribute
    An attribute describes an element's characteristics
Value
    A value identifies a specific characteristic

List Tags

There are several list tags:

- Ordered List **<ol> ... </ol>** This is used to set up an ordered list. Put <ol> at the start of the list and </ol> at the end of the list.
- Unordered List **<ul> ... </ul>** This is used to set up an unordered list. Put <ul> at the start of the list and </ul> at the end of the list.
- Definition List **<dl>... </dl>** This is used to set up a definition list. Put <dl> at the start of the list and </dl> at the end of the list.
- List item **<li>... </li>** This tag marks each item in an ordered or unordered list.

- Definition item **<dt>... </dt>** This tag marks each definition item in the list.
- Definition data **<dd>... </dd>** This tag marks the corresponding definition data in the list.

Here is an **ordered** list:

```
<ol>
<li>Rodgers Rop (Kenya)</li>
<li>Chris Cheboiboch (Kenya)</li>
<li>Fred Kiprop (Kenya)</li>
</ol>
```

In ordered lists you can use the 'type' attribute to select Roman or alphabetic labels. You can also use the 'start' attribute to set the initial value.

```
<ol type="I" start="5">
<li>Mike</li>
<li>Alan</li>
<li>Kevin</li>
</ol>
```

   V.   Mike
  VI.   Alan
 VII.   Kevin

In unordered lists you can use the **'type'** attribute to select whether you want a square, circle or disc:

```
<ul>
<li type="square">Rt. Hon. Sir Joseph Porter, K.C.B,
First Lord of the Admiralty</li>
<li type="circle">Captain Corcoran, Commanding "H.M.S.
Pinafore"</li>
<li type="disc">Ralph Rackstraw, able seaman</li>
</ul>
```

1. Rt. Hon. Sir Joseph Porter, K.C.B, First Lord of the Admiralty
   - Captain Corcoran, Commanding "H.M.S. Pinafore"

- Ralph Rackstraw, able seaman

Here is a definition list example:

```
<dl>
<dt>Bumboat</dt>
<dd>Boat used to peddle provisions to ships in
port.</dd>
<dt>Conies</dt>
<dd>Wild rabbits.</dd>
<dt>Grog</dt>
<dd>Rum diluted with water.</dd>
</dl>
```

Bumboat
     Boat used to peddle provisions to ships in port.
Conies
     Wild rabbits.
Grog
     Rum diluted with water.

Anchor Tag

The anchor tag **<a>** is used to provide a hyper-text link between two anchor points in the text. A source anchor point will link to a destination or bookmark anchor point. The text of the source anchor tag will appear underlined on the E-Book page.

Anchor tags are typically used in a Table of Contents where each entry in the Table of Contents has a source anchor tag that references a destination anchor tag at a section or chapter in the E-Book. The source anchor in the Table of Contents has a **href** attribute with the value of the destination anchor that it is referencing. A hash (#) character must precede the value of the **href** attribute as shown below.

```
<a href="#chapter-3">Chapter 3</a>
```

The destination anchor point at the chapter title has a **name** attribute:

```
<a name="chapter-3"><h4>Chapter 3</h4></a>
```

When you write your E-Book you can organize it as a single HTML file, or split it up into several HTML files, one for each chapter.

If you have several files that make up your E-Book you can create a separate Table of Contents HTML file that has hyperlinks to each chapter of your E-Book. The Table of Contents HTML file will have the HTML source anchor tags that link to a destination anchor tags in each chapter file as shown below. Note that <p> and </p> tags enclose each entry in the table of contents to ensure that they appear on separate lines.

```
<body>

<h1><a name="toc">Table of Contents</a></h1>

<p>
<a href="chapter1.html#start"><p>Chapter 1 Title</p></a>
<a href="chapter2.html#start"><p>Chapter 2 Title</p></a>
<a href="chapter3.html#start"><p>Chapter 3 Title</p></a>
<a href="chapter4.html#start"><p>Chapter 4 Title</p></a>
<a href="chapter5.html#start"><p>Chapter 5 Title</p></a>
<a href="chapter6.html#start"><p>Chapter 6 Title</p></a>
...
</p>

</body>
```

Figure 8 Table of Contents HTML File

Each HTML chapter file contains a destination anchor tag with a name attribute of 'start' that includes the chapter heading tag as shown below. For example the HTML file for chapter 3 would contain the anchor tag shown below.

```
<a name="start"><h1>Chapter 3 Title</h1></a>
```

When the reader taps on the link in the Table of Contents for a specific chapter, the E-Book reader device will link to that chapter heading and display that page.

Entities

Some characters such as less than (**<**) or greater than (**>**) are reserved in HTML for use as tag delimiters, so it not possible to use them in your text. To actually display reserved characters, HTML character entities must be used in the HTML source code. Entities are special instructions to the browser just like tags. They always start with an ampersand (**&**) followed by the entity name and then followed by a semi-colon. For example, the **÷** entity is used to display the ÷ symbol.

```
10 &divide; 2 = 5
```

is displayed as 10 ÷ 2 = 5

Entities describe special symbols that the browser should draw on the screen, such as math symbols, and letters with a foreign language accent such as an acute and a circumflex.

Entity	Symbol	Example
÷	÷	10÷2=5
<	<	2<7
>	>	8>5
é	é	gravé
ô	ô	rôle

Figure 9 HTML Entities

Tables

Currently the Kindle and the Nook do not provide good support for tables. HTML tables end up being virtually unreadable. It is recommended that you use images for your tables. The tables can be created by an image editor such as GIMP and inserted into your HTML document using the **<img>** tag.

CSS

CSS can be very useful in achieving a consistent appearance to things like chapter and section headings. For example, by specifying the properties of HTML heading tags , e.g., h0, h1, etc. you can control the appearance of the headings in your document. CSS statements are placed in the style section of your HTML document.

For example, if all h2 headings are to be bold, black, underlined and 18 point, and all h3 headings are to be bold, black and 14 point, then the properties in the style section can be declared as:

```
<style>
h2 {
   font-weight: bold;
   color: black;
   font-size: 18pt;
   text-decoration:underline;
}

h3 {
   font-weight: bold;
   color: black;
   font-size: 14pt;
}
</style>
```

Figure 10 HTML Style Section

3 Organizing the Contents

The contents of the E-Book are arranged into chapters and paragraphs within the **<body>** section.

Body Layout

The content for the E-Book is placed in the **<body>** section. The content of a book such as a novel consists of text divided into paragraphs and chapters. The HTML layout for the E-Book in the **<body>** section will therefore consist of a set of chapters defined by heading tags containing paragraphs as shown below:

```
<body>

<h1>Chapter 1</h1>
<p>First paragraph for chapter 1</p>
<p>Next paragraph for chapter 1</p>
...

<h1>Chapter 2</h1>
<p>First paragraph for chapter 2</p>
<p>Next paragraph for chapter 2</p>
...

<h1>Chapter 3</h1>
<p>First paragraph for chapter 3</p>
<p>Next paragraph for chapter 3</p>
...

</body>
```

Figure 11 E-Book Body Layout

For an E-Book that has more hierarchical structure of sections and sub-sections, the HTML layout for the E-Book will consist of several levels of heading tags containing paragraphs as shown below. The **<h1>** tag is used for section headings and the **<h2>** tag is used for sub-section headings.

```
<body>
```

```
<h1>1 Section A</h1>
<p>First paragraph for section 1</p>
<p>Next paragraph for section 1</p>
...

<h2>1.1 Sub-section</h2>
<p>First paragraph for sub-section 1.1</p>
<p>Next paragraph for section 1.1</p>
...

<h2>1.2 Sub-section</h2>
<p>First paragraph for sub-section 1.2</p>
<p>Next paragraph for section 1.2</p>
...

<h1>2 Section B</h1>
<p>First paragraph for section 2</p>
<p>Next paragraph for section 2</p>
...
<h2>2.1 Sub-section</h2>
<p>First paragraph for sub-section 2.1</p>
<p>Next paragraph for section 2.1</p>
...

</body>
```

Figure 12 Hierarchical Heading Tags

Book Organization

Your book will consist of a number of chapters as well as a title section, a preface or introduction, a table of contents, and maybe an index, glossary or appendices. Each of these should be placed in a separate HTML document. These separate documents are then added to the book project you will create in the one of the tools, such as MobiPocket Creator or Calibre, that convert HTML to the MOBI or EPUB formatted files required by Amazon KDP and Nook Press.

An example of each of these is shown below. The text in bold is what you would need to modify for your E-Book.

Title Section

This HTML file contains the E-Book title with a sub-title, the author and the copyright.

```
<?xml version="1.0" encoding="utf-8" standalone="no"?>
<!DOCTYPE html PUBLIC "-//W3C//DTD XHTML 1.1//EN"
   "http://www.w3.org/TR/xhtml11/DTD/xhtml11.dtd">

<html        xmlns="http://www.w3.org/1999/xhtml"        xml:lang="en"
xmlns:xsi="http://www.w3.org/2001/XMLSchema-instance">
<head>
 <title>My E-Book</title>
 <link href="../Styles/styles.css" rel="stylesheet" type="text/css"
>
 <meta http-equiv="Content-Type" content="text/html; charset=UTF-8"
/>

<style type="text/css">


</style>
</head>

<body>

<h1 align=center>My Book Title</h1>

<p align=center >An epic saga of the old West</p>
<p align=center >By</p>
<p align=center >Joe Brown</p>

<p align=center >Copyright &copy; 2012 by Joe Brown</p>

</body>
</html>
```

Figure 13 HTML File for the Title section

Table of Contents

Each entry in the table of contents will have a HTML source anchor tag that links to a destination anchor tag in each chapter file. In this example the anchor tags have the name attribute of "start" as shown below.

```
<?xml version="1.0" encoding="utf-8" standalone="no"?>
<!DOCTYPE html PUBLIC "-//W3C//DTD XHTML 1.1//EN"
   "http://www.w3.org/TR/xhtml11/DTD/xhtml11.dtd">
```

```
<html        xmlns="http://www.w3.org/1999/xhtml"        xml:lang="en"
xmlns:xsi="http://www.w3.org/2001/XMLSchema-instance">
<head>
 <title>My E-Book</title>
 <link href="../Styles/styles.css" rel="stylesheet" type="text/css"
>
 <meta http-equiv="Content-Type" content="text/html; charset=UTF-8"
/>

<style type="text/css">


</style>
</head>

<body>

<h1><a name="toc">Table of Contents</a></h1>

<p>
<a href="chapter1.html#start"><p>Chapter 1 Title</p></a>
<a href="chapter2.html#start"><p>Chapter 2 Title</p></a>
<a href="chapter3.html#start"><p>Chapter 3 Title</p></a>
<a href="chapter4.html#start"><p>Chapter 4 Title</p></a>
<a href="chapter5.html#start"><p>Chapter 5 Title</p></a>
<a href="chapter6.html#start"><p>Chapter 6 Title</p></a>
</p>

</body>
</html>
```

Figure 14 Table of Contents

Chapters

Each chapter can be put in a separate HTML file. Each HTML chapter file contains a destination anchor tag with a name attribute of "start" that encloses the chapter heading as shown below. This will link the chapter item in the Table of Contents file to this chapter heading in this chapter file.

```
<?xml version="1.0" encoding="utf-8" standalone="no"?>
<!DOCTYPE html PUBLIC "-//W3C//DTD XHTML 1.1//EN"
   "http://www.w3.org/TR/xhtml11/DTD/xhtml11.dtd">

<html xmlns="http://www.w3.org/1999/xhtml" xml:lang="en"
xmlns:xsi="http://www.w3.org/2001/XMLSchema-instance">
<head>
 <title>My E-Book</title>
 <link href="../Styles/styles.css" rel="stylesheet"
type="text/css" >
```

```
 <meta http-equiv="Content-Type" content="text/html; charset=UTF-
8" />

<style type="text/css">


</style>
</head>

<body>

<a name="start"><h1>Chapter 1 Title</h1></a>

<p>First paragraph for chapter 1</p>
<p>Next paragraph for chapter 1</p>
...

</body>
</html>
```

Figure 15 HTML for a Chapter

4 Images

You will need an image for the E-Book's cover and possibly also any pictures or illustrations you want to include within the content of the book. You will also want to use an image for any tables that you have in your E-Book. You may also need to make thumbnail images that can be used on the sales page for your E-Book.

The dimensions and resolution for images to be included in an E-Book are specified by the E-Book publishers.

Creating the Cover

A well designed, good looking cover is the key to selling your E-Book. Your cover needs to have an eye-catching appearance that invites your potential reader to take the next step of looking inside your E-Book as they browse the E-Bookstore.

You can design you own cover or get someone to design it for you. If you don't feel comfortable doing your own design you can use job search sites such as `fiverr.com` to get a cover designer to do it for you. Post a description of what you have in mind for the cover and hire a contract designer to do the work for you.

KDP also offers the Cover Creator tool which will allow you create your own cover using a pre-selected set of images.
Once you have your cover image in the form of a JPEG file you can upload it to the book publication page for the Kindle or the Nook.

Using GIMP

To edit pictures use a digital image editor such as Adobe PhotoShop or GIMP. The GNU Image Manipulation Program (GIMP) has the advantage in that it is free. GIMP is an open source program that you can download and use to edit your images. This program is very useful and has most features that you would need for processing images for an E-Book. GIMP can be downloaded from `http://www.gimp.org/`.

GIMP is a very sophisticated tool that can be used for various tasks such as enhancing digital photographs.

The basics of GIMP are quite straightforward. GIMP allows you to import images, make changes to them, scale them, resize them and make other enhancements, and then export them in a desired format. GIMP supports a wide variety of formats including JPEG which is required for Kindle and Nook. For more details on how to use GIMP to create E-Book covers and edit other images, read the book 'GIMP for Book Publishers and Authors'.

Image Capture

For some books you may want to capture an image from your computer. For Windows you can press the **Fn** key with the **PrtSc** (Print Screen) key to copy the entire screen to the clipboard. You can then paste that image into your document or into GIMP for further editing. To copy just the active window press the **Fn** key, the **Alt** key and **PrtSc** key.

The Snipping Tool can also be used to capture screen shots. It offers the following options:

- Free-form Snip. Draw any shape around an object with your finger, mouse, or tablet pen.
- Rectangular Snip. Drag the cursor around an object to form a rectangle.
- Window Snip. Choose a window—like a browser window or a dialog box.
- Full-screen Snip. Capture the entire screen.

5 Publishing for the Kindle

Publishing for the Kindle is done on at Amazon's Kindle Direct Publishing (KDP). Publishing an E-Book for the Kindle involves several steps:

1. Create a new book on the KDP website.
2. Edit HTML files with a text editor to create the E-Book content.
3. Create the E-Book cover and edit any image files with GIMP.
4. Import the HTML files and the images files into Mobipocket Creator to build the MOBI format E-Book document.
5. Upload the MOBI document to KDP for publication.
6. Initiate the publication of your E-Book on KDP.

This process of creating a MOBI format file that can be uploaded to KDP is summarized below.

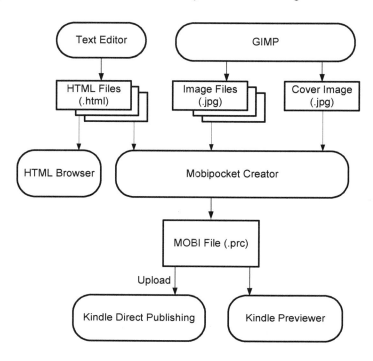

Figure 16 MOBI File Creation

Tools

The following tools are needed to format an E-Book for Kindle reader devices:

1. HTML Editor. Use jEdit or TextPad to edit your E-Book.
2. HTML Browser. Open the HTML file from a browser such as Firefox or Internet Explorer to view the HTML file.
3. Mobipocket Creator. You can use Mobipocket Creator to convert your HTML document to the MOBI format file that you can upload to Amazon's Kindle Direct Publishing for publication. The Mobipocket Creator is described in the next chapter.

4. Kindle Previewer to view your E-Book. While you are creating your E-Book it is useful to be able to view your E-Book as it would appear on a Kindle reader device.

Kindle Previewer

The Kindle Previewer will let you view the Kindle E-Book. The Kindle Previewer emulates a number of devices including the Kindle, Kindle Fire, Kindle DX, Kindle for iPad and Kindle for iPhone.

The Kindle Previewer can be downloaded from:

`http://www.amazon.com/gp/feature.html?docId=1000765261`

The Kindle Previewer User's Guide can be downloaded from:

`http://kindlepreviewer.s3.amazonaws.com/UserGuide.pdf`

Figure 17 Kindle Previewer

The Kindle Previewer will display your E-Book as it would appear on various Kindle E-Book readers. You can select different orientations, fonts and font sizes. You should browse through your E-Book and evaluate its appearance. Make changes to your HTML files until you are satisfied with the result.

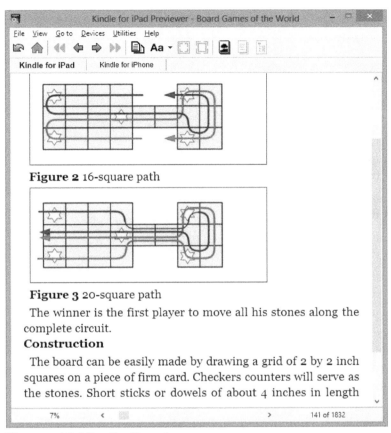

Figure 18 Kindle Previewer

Kindle Direct Publishing

To get started publishing on Kindle you need to open an account at Amazon's Kindle Direct Publishing (KDP) which can be found at **https://kdp.amazon.com**. You will need to enter your bank account number and social security number or tax identification number.

Figure 19 Kindle Direct Publishing

These days most people have an Amazon account. Log in and you will arrive at the main KDP page. Listed across the top are other available pages including:

- Bookshelf. This will list all the books you have published. It will not show any books initially. This is where you manage your E-Books. You can add new titles, upload cover images, set pricing of your E-Book, and upload new editions.
- Reports. This lists your sales on a daily and monthly basis. Your payments are also available from this page.
- Community. This gives you access to the KDP community where you can find lots of information about publishing on the Kindle.
- KDP Select. This is a promotional program that you can use to enhance your sales. If you enroll in this program you will earn a share of the KDP Select Global fund when readers borrow your books from the Kindle Owner's

Lending Library (KOLL). You will see these payments marked as KOLL under Prior Months Reports.

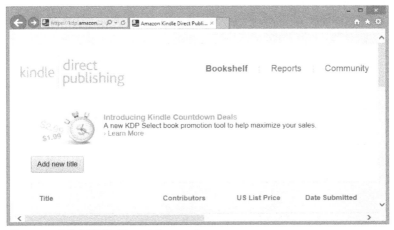

Figure 20 KDP Dashboard

Steps to Take

Here is a quick summary of what you need to do.

1. Start the process by adding a new title for your E-Book in the Bookshelf page.
2. Enter the E-Book's title, description and search keywords.
3. Upload the JPEG file for the book cover.
4. Upload the E-Book content file.
5. Check the appearance of your E-Book using Amazon's online viewer.
6. Select the distribution, pricing and royalty of your E-Book.
7. Click Save and Publish.

8. Amazon will check that your E-Book meets their publishing criteria and email you when the book is ready.

This is a straight forward process. Once published you check your E-Book sales in the Reports page. Let's go through the publishing process in more detail.

Adding a new Title

To start new book, click on the 'Add new title' button. This will take you to a new page where you can start to enter information about your book.

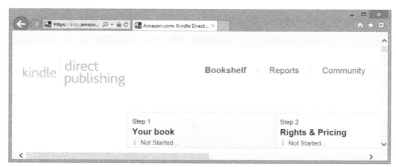

Figure 21 Add a New Title

Book Details

Scroll down to where you can enter details about your book including its title, sub-title, whether it is part of a series and the edition number (just enter 1).

Figure 22 Book Details

Book Description

Further down you get to enter the publisher (yourself), a description of the book and author, language, publication date and ISBN. The description will appear on the Amazon sales page for the E-Book so it is important for you to capture the essence of what your E-Book is about.

You don't need an ISBN for E-Books so leave that box empty. Instead Amazon will assign your E-Book a unique 10-digit ASIN (Amazon Standard Identification Number).

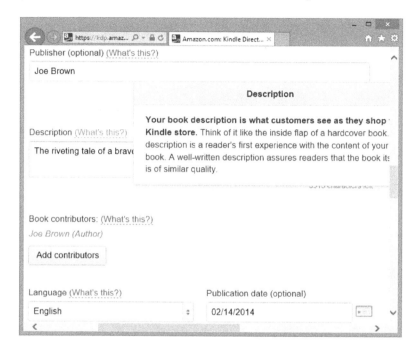

Figure 23 Book Description

Publishing Rights

Now you need to select your publishing rights. If you wrote the content then click on 'This is not a public domain work and I hold the necessary publishing rights'.

Target Customers

Next you target your customers by first selecting the category in which they can find your E-Book and choosing keywords that can be used to search for your E-Book. Think about the setting of the book, the type and role of main character, and the plot when selecting the keywords. For example the setting may be the Old West, the main character may be a mountain man and the plot may be an epic quest.

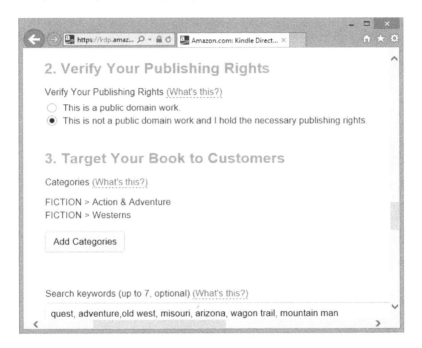

Figure 24 Publishing Rights and Categories

Front Cover

The next thing you need to do is to design the front cover. You can design you own cover or get someone to design it for you. Once you have your cover image in the form of a JPEG file you can upload it to the KDP book page.

KDP also offers the Cover Creator tool which will allow you to select form a number of background and layout designs, color schemes and fonts.

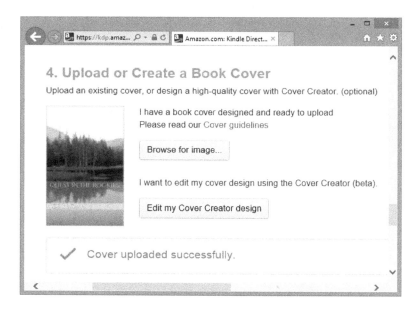

Figure 25 Upload a Cover

Content

Now you upload the MOBI-formatted content file. Browse for the file on your computer and upload it. KDP will run a spell check against the uploaded content and this gives you a chance to correct any errors in the content and upload again. You may find that you have to upload the book several times before you have the layout exactly as you want.

Figure 26 Upload content file

Review Your E-Book

The next step is to review your E-Book. You will have previously done this using the Kindle Previewer but you should do it again to verify that the content file that you uploaded to the KDP site is correct. Upload the content again after you have correctly any problems.

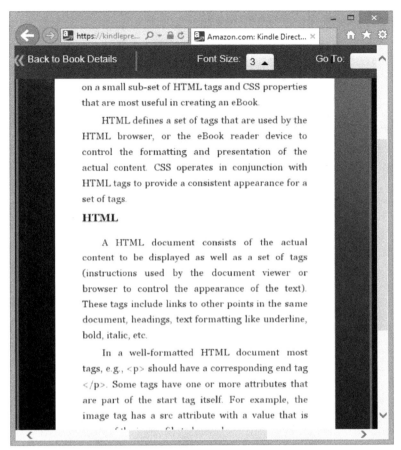

Figure 27 Review E-Book

Next you need to select your publishing territories. Choose worldwide so you can get as wide a distribution as possible.

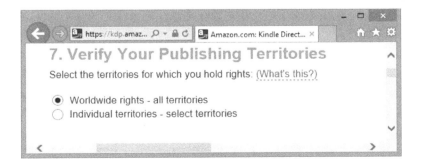

Figure 28 Publishing Territories

Pricing and Royalty

Select your pricing and royalty. KDP offers either 35% or 70% royalty. To select 70% royalty the book must be priced between $2.99 and $9.99.

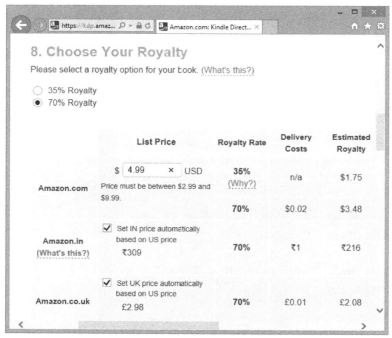

Figure 29 KDP Pricing and Royalties

You will also need to enter your bank account and routing number in your KDP account settings menu to have the royalties deposited into your bank account. Royalties are typically paid 60 days after the end of the month in which the book sales occurred. You will receive an email indicating that the funds have been deposited into your account.

Publish

Finally you request that your E-Book be published on Amazon. The content of your E-Book will now be reviewed by KDP staff. This usually takes about 24 hours. You will receive an email when this is complete. Included in the email is a link to the page where your book appears live on the Amazon bookstore. There is also a link from each E-Book item on the Bookshelf page to the E-Book listing on the Amazon.com Bookstore.

Figure 30 Publishing the E-Book

Reports

At the top of the main dashboard is a link to Reports. This will list the sales of your book in various categories. You can view these reports for the Amazon.com bookstore as well as individual country bookstores such as Amazon.co.uk.

- Sales Dashboard. The Sales Dash board provides a graph of sales over a selectable time period. You can filter by marketplace and title.
- Month-to-Date Unit Sales are updated on a daily basis.
- Prior Six Weeks' Royalties are updated every Saturday night.

- Prior Months' Royalties are generated on the 15th of the month. You can download an Excel spreadsheet for each month that shows the sales in each country.
- Promotions. This lists activity of your Kindle Countdown Deals.
- Payments. This lists the payments made to your bank account.

Figure 31 Reports Page

Amazon KDP also offers a Kindle Owners Lending Library (KOLL) where customers can check out your E-Book. You are paid for each time your E-Book is borrowed.

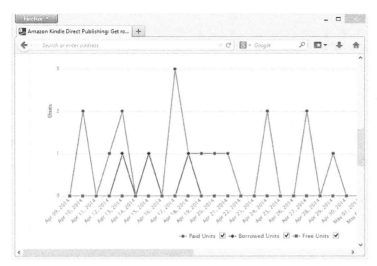

Figure 32 Graphical Sales Dashboard

6 Mobipocket Creator

To publish an E-Book for the Kindle, you need to use the Mobipocket Creator. This program lets you import the HTML files of your E-Book and convert them to a single Kindle MOBI format file. Each E-Book is managed as a separate publication in Mobipocket Creator.

When you start Mobipocket Creator you will see the main window shown below.

Figure 33 Mobipocket Creator

Download and Installation

Mobipocket Creator is freely available for download. Mobipocket Creator can be downloaded from:

`http://www.mobipocket.com/en/downloadsoft/productdetailscreator.asp`

For Windows the installer will run and allow you to select the folder in which the Mobipocket Creator files are to be placed.

There is a tutorial to using Mobipocket Creator at:

`http://www.mobipocket.com/en/DownloadSoft/tutorial.asp?Language=EN`

Using Mobipocket Creator

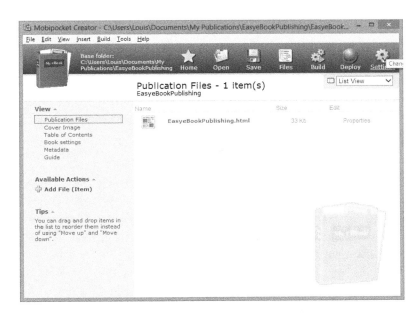

Figure 34 Mobipocket Publication

Follow these steps to create an E-Book using Mobipocket Creator:

1. Edit the HTML file. Put all the image files into a separate sub-folder.
2. Start Mobipocket Creator.
3. Select the folder you will use for the publication by clicking on the **Settings** icon at the top right. This folder will contain all the HTML files that are added to the publication as well as all MOBI files created by Mobipocket Creator. Click **Update** when you have made your changes.

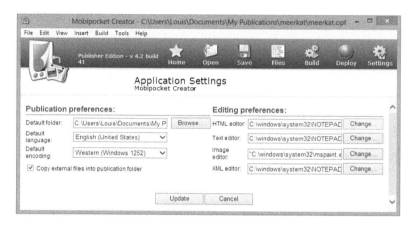

Figure 35 Mobipocket Setting Menu

4. Add the HTML files to Mobipocket Creator, by clicking on **Add File** under Available Actions on the left hand panel. As you add the HTML files you can re-arrange their order in the Publication panel using the up and down arrows as shown below.

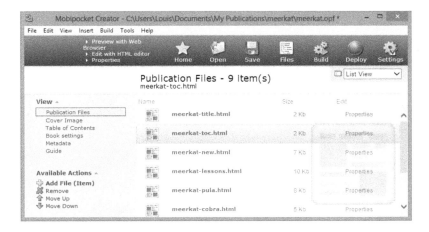

Figure 36 Mobipocket HTML File Ordering

5. Insert the cover image by clicking on **Cover Image** on the View panel at the left and select the image file from your image sub-folder. Your will see the image appear in the main Mobipocket Creator panel. Now click the **Update** button.

Figure 37 Insert Cover Image

6. Add the metadata information for the publication by clicking on Metadata in the View panel.

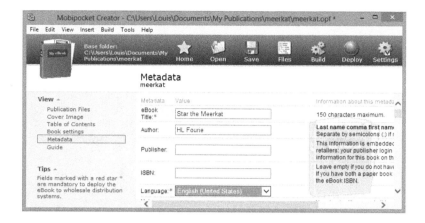

Figure 38 E-Book Metadata

Enter the E-Book title, author, publisher and description. When you are done click the **Update** button at the bottom.

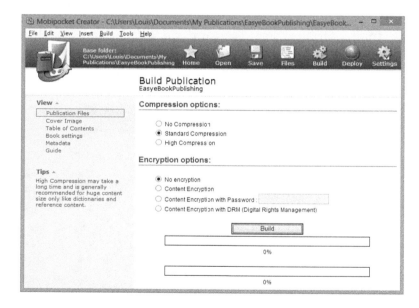

Figure 39 Mobipocket Build

On the Build Publication page, select standard compression and no encryption for the build and then click on the **Build** button to create the MOBI file. The status of the build will be shown on the progress bars.

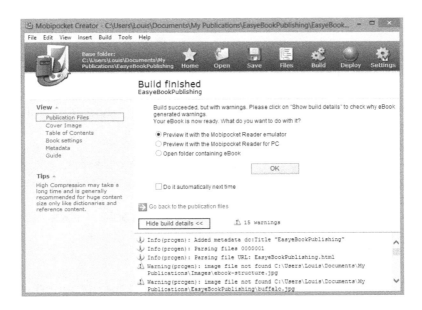

Figure 40 Mobipocket Build Complete

When the build completes it will list notifications and warnings of problems that may have occurred during the build such as a missing image file. You will find the final MOBI file with a .prc extension in the publication folder.

This is the MOBI file that you will upload to KDP for publication. You can also view this MOBI formatted E-Book using the Kindle Previewer.

7 Publishing for the Nook

To publish an E-Book for the Nook you need to perform the following steps:

1. Create your E-Book using an HTML text editor. You will likely have several HTML files for the title page, table of contents, the chapters, appendixes and glossary.
2. Create the E-Book cover and edit any image files with GIMP.
3. Assemble the HTML files and image files and convert them to an EPUB document using Sigil or Calibre.
4. Create a new E-Book on Nook Press and enter all the details.
5. Upload the EPUB document to Nook Press for publication.
6. Initiate publication on Nook Press.

This process of creating an EPUB file that can be uploaded to Nook Press is summarized below.

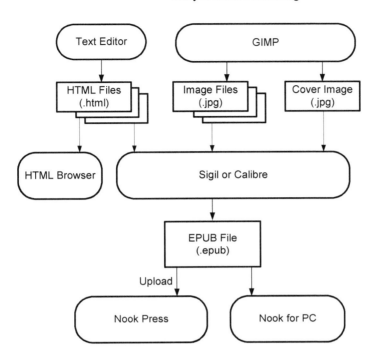

Figure 41 EPUB Creation Process

Tools

The following tools are needed to publish a book for the Nook reader:

1. HTML Editor. Use jEdit or TextPad to edit your E-Book.
2. HTML Browser. Open the HTML file from a browser such as Firefox or Internet Explorer to view the HTML file.
3. EPUB Convertor. You can use Calibre or Sigil to convert your HTML document to an EPUB file that you can upload to Nook Press for publication.
4. Nook for PC to view your E-Book.

If you have the contents for your book in Word or PDF format, then first convert to an HTML file.

Nook Format

Nook reader devices use the EPUB format.

Nook for PC

The Nook for PC E-Book reader program will let you view the EPUB E-Book on your own computer. The Nook for PC lets you read the EPUB document so that it appears in same way as reading on an actual Nook reading device.

Nook for PC for a computer running Windows 7 can be downloaded from:

`http://www.barnesandnoble.com/u/nook-for-pc/379003591/`

Nook for Windows 8 can be downloaded from:

`http://www.barnesandnoble.com/u/nook-for-windows-8/379003757`

Nook for Mac can be downloaded from:

`http://www.barnesandnoble.com/u/nook-for-mac/379003592/`

Figure 42 Nook for PC

Follow these steps to load your E-Book into Nook for PC. First click on **my library > my stuff** item, and then click on the **Add New Item** button at the top of the window. An Add File dialog will appear. Enter the name of the EPUB file for your E-Book and clock on **Open**. Your E-book will appear in your library as shown below.

Figure 43 Nook for PC add New Item

Now click on the item in your E-Book to read it. It will now be displayed as it would on a Nook E-Book reader.

All the E-Books that are added to the library are stored in a folder called My Barnes & Noble eBooks. You will find that if you try to add the same E-Book to the library again, if you have review any changes that you have made, an error message appears saying that this file has already been added to the library. In this case delete the old file from the folder My Barnes & Noble eBooks and start Nook for PC again.

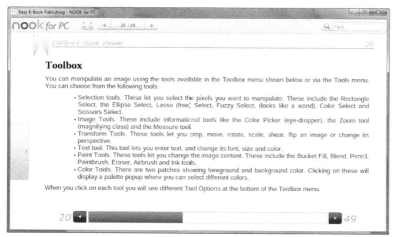

Figure 44 Reading an E-Book using Nook for PC

There is a progress bar at the bottom of the page to show your position in the E-Book.

Publishing on Nook Press

To get started publishing for the Nook you need to open an account at the Nook Press home page which can be found at `www.nookpress.com`.

Figure 45 Nook Press

You will also need to enter your bank account and routing number in your Nook Press account settings menu to have the royalties deposited into your bank account. Royalties are typically paid 60 days after the end of the month in which the book sales occurred. You will receive an email indicating that the funds have been deposited into your account.

Once you have created your Nook Press account you will arrive at the Nook Press dashboard shown below. Listed across the top are other available pages including:

- Projects. This page will list all the books you have published. It will not show any books initially. This is where you manage your E-Books. You can add new titles, upload cover images, set pricing of your E-Book, and upload new editions.

- Sales. This page lists your daily and monthly sales as well as payments.
- Support. This page gives you access to a wide variety of information about publishing on Nook Press.
- News. This is a promotional program that you can use to enhance your sales.

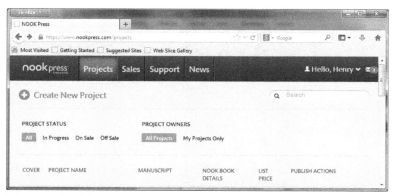

Figure 46 Nook Press Dashboard

Here is a quick summary of what you need to do.

1. Sign in to your Nook Press account at www.nookpress.com.
2. Enter your bank account and tax information to receive royalties.
3. Start the process by adding a new title for your E-Book in the Projects page.
4. Enter the E-Book's title, description and search keywords.
5. Upload the JPEG file for the book cover.
6. Upload the EPUB content file.
7. Check the appearance of your E-Book using the Nook for PC viewer.
8. Select the distribution, pricing and royalty of your E-Book.
9. Click Save and Publish.

10. Nook Press will check that your E-Book meets their publishing criteria and email you when the book is ready.

This is a straight forward process. Once published, you can check your E-Book sales on the Sales page. Let's go through the publishing process in more detail.

Adding a new Project

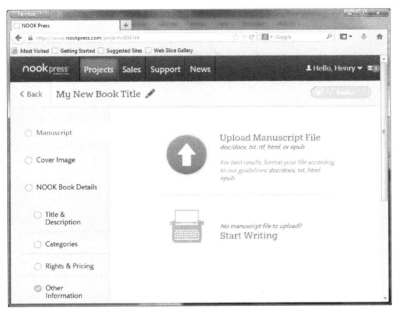

Figure 47 Add New Project

To start new book, click on the 'Create New Project' button. This will take you to a new page where you can start to enter information about your book.

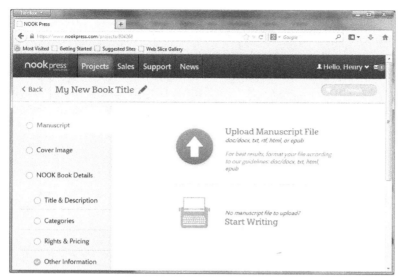

Figure 48 New Project

Upload Manuscript

Now you upload the manuscript for your E-book. Browse for the EPUB file on your computer and upload it. You may find that you have to upload the book several times before you have the layout exactly as you want. Once you have done this, the Project page for your E-book will appear as shown below.

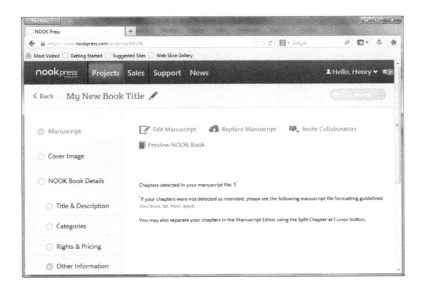

Figure 49 Upload Manuscript

Book Details

Click on Title & Description to enter details about your E-book including its title, publisher, publication date and author's name.

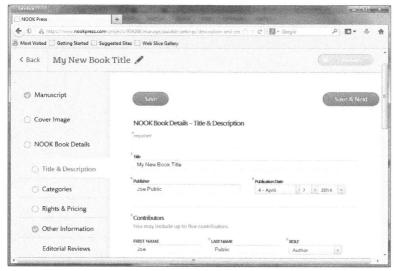

Figure 50 Book Details

Book Description

Scroll down you get to enter the description of the E-book and author, and ISBN. The description will appear on the Barnes & Noble sales page for the E-Book so it is important for you to capture the essence of what your E-Book is about.

You don't need an ISBN for E-Books so leave that box empty.

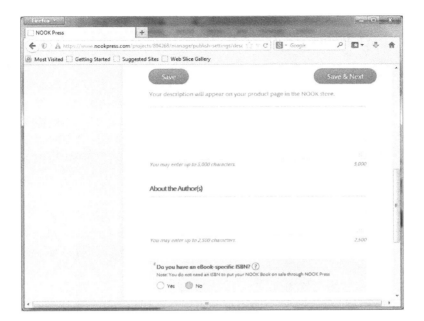

Figure 51 Book Description

Now you need to select your publishing rights. If you wrote the content then click on 'This is not a public domain work and I hold the necessary publishing rights'.

Use Categories to Target Customers

Next you target your customers by first selecting the category in which they can find your E-Book and choosing keywords that can be used to search for your E-Book. Think about the setting of the book, the type and role of main character, and the plot when selecting the keywords. Select also your target audience and the language of the E-book.

Figure 52 Categories to target customers

Pricing and Royalty

Next you need to select your publishing territories. Choose worldwide so you can get as wide a distribution as possible. Select your pricing and get an estimate of your royalty.

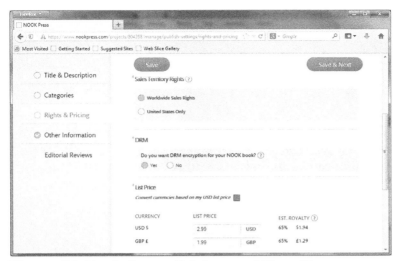

Figure 53 Nook Press Pricing and Royalties

Other Information

Other information you need to enter includes whether your E-book is in the public domain, is part of a series, and is it already available in print.

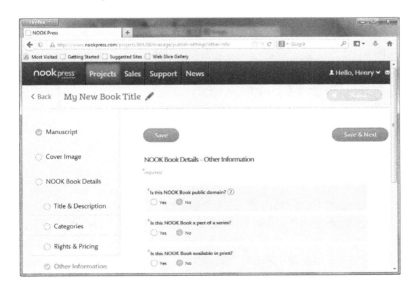

Figure 54 Other Information

Front Cover

The next thing you need to do is to design the front cover. You can design you own cover or get someone to design it for you. Once you have your cover image in the form of a JPEG file you can upload it to Nook Press.

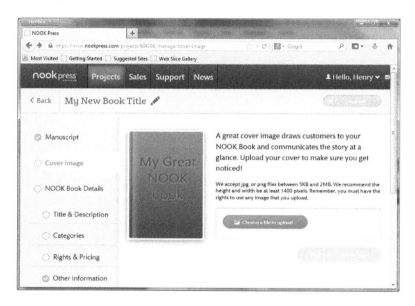

Figure 55 Nook Press Cover Upload

Publish

Finally you request that your E-Book be published on Barnes & Noble. The content of your E-Book will now be reviewed by their staff. This usually takes about 24 hours. You will receive an email when this is complete. Included in the email is a link to the page where your book appears live on the bookstore.

Figure 56 Publish

Sales

At the top of the main dashboard is a link to Sales. This will list the sales of your book in various categories. You can view sales of your E-Books on the Barnes & Noble bookstore. You can get the following sales reports:

- Month-to-Date Unit Sales are updated on a daily basis.
- Previous month's Sales.
- Monthly Sales which you can download an Excel spreadsheet.
- Payments. This lists the payments made to your bank account.

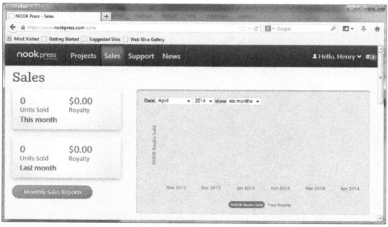

Figure 57 Nook Press Sales

Support

The Support link at the top of the main dashboard directs you to a page that provides a lot of information on creating, publishing and marketing your E-Book.

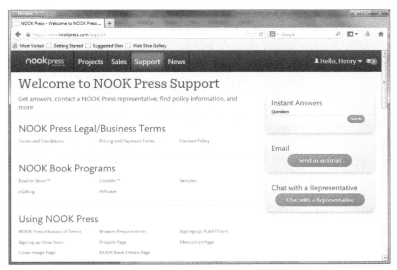

Figure 58 Nook Press Support

8 Sigil

To publish an E-Book for the Nook, you can use Sigil to convert the HTML-formatted material to an EPUB formatted E-Book. It allows you to edit your E-Book as you would view it on the Nook reader device and then save your E-Book in EPUB format. However, Sigil will accept HTML code but it will only save the HTML material as an EPUB document. If you want to save any work you have already done within Sigil, you cannot save those changes as a HTML file. The best approach is to do the following:

1. Edit your HTML material using a text editor and save those changes within the text editor.
2. Read the HTML document into Sigil using Open to add the cover images, table of contents and title information.
3. Save the document from Sigil as an EPUB document.

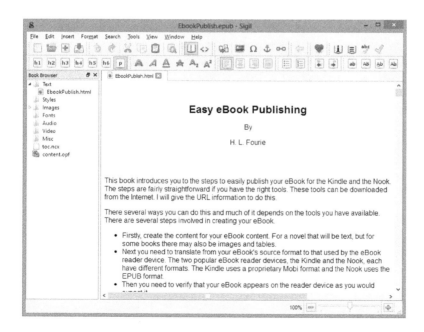

Figure 59 Sigil E-Book Editor

Download and Installation

Sigil has been developed as an open source project by Google and is freely available for download. Sigil can be downloaded from:

`http://code.google.com/p/sigil/`

There is a list of Sigil downloads for Linux, Mac and Windows at:

`http://code.google.com/p/sigil/downloads/list`

Download the right file for your computer.

The installation instructions for Sigil are at:

`http://code.google.com/p/sigil/wiki/InstallationInstructions`

For Windows the installer will run and allow you to select the folder in which the Sigil files are to be placed.

There is a complete User's Guide at:

`http://web.sigil.googlecode.com/git/contents.html`

Using Sigil

Follow these steps to edit an E-Book and convert the HTML file to EPUB format using Sigil:

1. Edit the HTML file. Put all the image files into a separate sub-folder.

2. Start Sigil.
3. Open the HTML file from Sigil, click on **File > Open**.

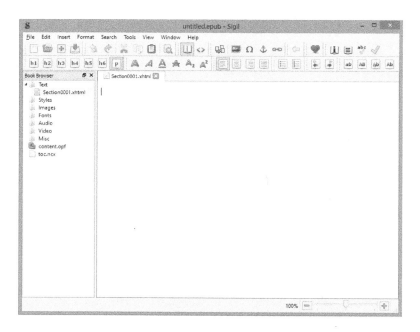

Figure 60 Open HTML document in Sigil

4. Add additional HTML files for each chapter as shown below. The HTML files appear in the Text section of the left hand panel as they are added. You can re-order the chapters by selecting one of the HTML files and dragging to the desired position.

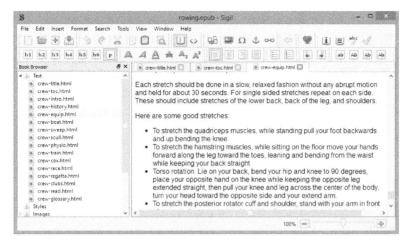

Figure 61 HTML Files in Sigil E-Book

4. You can switch between the code view and the book view of an HTML file by clicking on the Code View and Book View icons on the Toolbar at the top of the window.

Figure 62 Sigil Code View

5. Insert the cover image: move the cursor to the start of the document in the main Sigil pane and click on **Insert > Image** and select the image file from your image sub-folder. Your will see the image appear in the main Sigil pane. Next, insert a chapter break by clicking on **Insert > Chapter Break**.

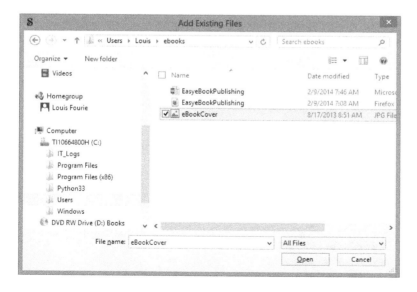

Figure 63 Insert cover image

6. All the images included in the E-Book appear in the images folder as shown below.

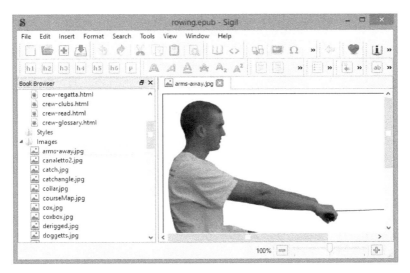

Figure 64 Sigil Images

7. Insert a Table of Contents: in the Table of Contents panel, click on **Headings > Generate TOC**. This panel allows you to select the headings that you want to include in your Table of Contents.

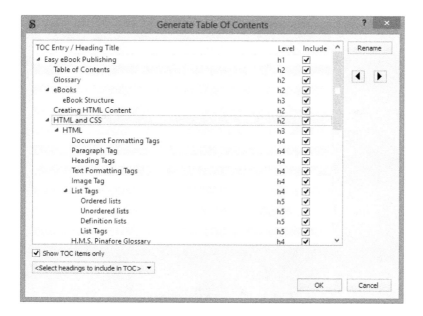

Figure 65 Insert Table of Contents

Save as an EPUB document: click on **File > Save As** and select the name of the EPUB document. As mentioned before Sigil can only save a document as an EPUB formatted E-Book.

You can now read your EPUB document using the Nook for PC E-Book reader and when satisfied with its appearance you can upload it to Nook Press.

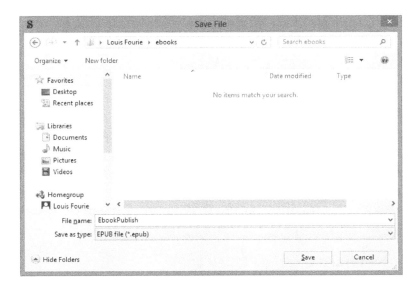

Figure 66 Save as EPUB document in Sigil

8. Verify that the E-Book has the desired appearance. Check how it appears with different fonts and font sizes. Jump to different pages in your E-Book. You will likely need to repeat the previous steps to correct any problems that you have found.

9 Calibre

Calibre is a very useful tool for managing a library of E-Books. It can also be used to convert between different E-Book formats and downloading E-Books to reader devices. Calibre is a free open source E-Book library management application. Calibre also includes an E-Book viewer. Calibre will let you import your HTML document and then convert it to an EPUB or MOBI document.

Help for using Calibre can be found at:

```
http://calibre-E-Book.com/help
```

Calibre provides some very useful videos to get you started at:

```
http://calibre-E-Book.com/demo
```

Tips on using Calibre can be found at:

```
http://www.teleread.com/drm/the-abcs-of-format-conversion-for-the-
kindle-sony-and-nook-plus-some-calibre-tips/
```

Download and Installation

Calibre has been developed as an open source project and is freely available for download. Calibre for Linux, Apple OS X and Windows can be downloaded from:

```
http://calibre-E-Book.com/download
```

Download the correct file for your computer and follow the installation instructions. For Windows the installer will run and allow you to select the folder in which the Calibre files are to be placed.

Using Calibre

Calibre consists of three separate programs:

1. E-book Library Manager
2. E-Book Editor
3. E-Book Viewer

Calibre E-Book Library Manager

The Calibre E-Book Manager lets you manage a library of E-Books. Calibre lets you add E-Books to your library collection and then search for an E-Book using various attributes such as author, language, format, publisher, size and rating, or certain metadata tags. Calibre will also retrieve metadata information from the Internet using an E-Book title, author or ISBN.

Calibre also converts between different E-Book formats. Calibre can interface with your E-Book reader device and download E-Books from the Calibre library to the reader.

Figure 67 Calibre E-Book Manager

You can add E-Books to the library and they will appear in the book list in the central panel of the window. There are icons at the bottom right of the main window that let you enable the display of the various panels on the main window:

- Book list. This is the list of all E-Books that have been added to the Calibre Library Manager appears as the central panel.
- Cover display. This displays the covers of the all E-Books in the library.
- Book details. This displays details of the book currently selected on the book list and appears as a right hand panel.
- Tags browser. This allows you to sort your E-Books using various tags such as author, language, format, publisher and rating.

You can select a book and change its metadata. The metadata for an E-Book includes its title, author and publication date which will be part of the EPUB-formatted or MOBI-formatted document created by Calibre.

Figure 68 Edit Metadata

Calibre lets you convert between different formats.

Figure 69 Format Conversion

Calibre E-Book Editor

When you start Calibre E-Book Editor the screen shown below will be displayed.

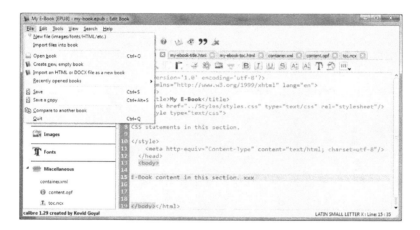

Figure 70 Calibre E-Book Editor

To open an HTML file from the Calibre, click on **File > Import an HTML or DOCX file as a new book**. The name of the HTML file will appear in the left hand panel under Text. Double-click on the file name to open it. The HTML file will be displayed in the center panel and the browser view will appear in the right hand panel.

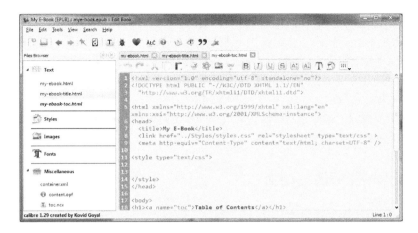

Figure 71 Editing an E-Book

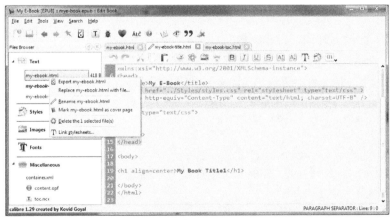

Figure 72 HTML File options

You can add more HTML files to the E-Book by clicking on **File > Import files into book**. These files will appear on the left hand panel also. Double-click on the file name to open it. You can then make changes to the HTML file. If you right-click on the HTML file in the Text panel a popup will appear with these options:

- Export. To save the HTML file.
- Replace. To replace this HTML file with another.
- Rename. To rename the HTML file
- Mark as cover page. To mark it as the cover page.
- Delete. To delete the HTML file.
- Link style sheets. To link the file to the CSS style sheets

Convert to EPUB format

To save your changes to an EPUB file, click on **File > Save a Copy**. This will create the EPUB file that you can upload to Nook Press.

Calibre E-Book Viewer

The E-Book Viewer let you view an E-Book as it would appear on an E-Book reader. Follow these steps to view an E-Book using the Calibre E-Book Viewer:

1. Start the Calibre E-Book Viewer
2. Open the HTML file from the E-Book Viewer, click on **Open ebook** icon.
3. Browse the E-Book and verify the presentation is as desired.

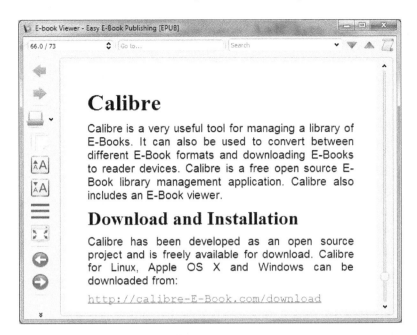

Figure 73 E-Book Viewer

You can configure the E-Book reading experience to change fonts, font sizes, and foreground and background colors by clicking on the Preferences icon on the left panel.

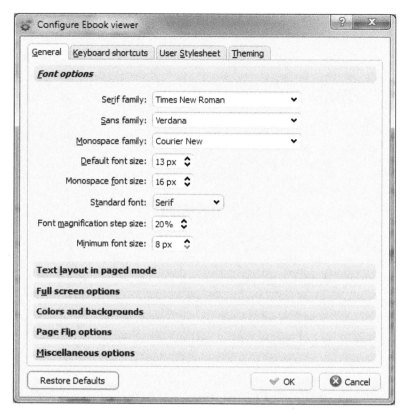

Figure 74 E-Book Viewer Preferences

10 Further Reading

Books

Here is a list of books that provide more information.

Peck, Akkana. 2006. *Beginning GIMP*, Apress

Van Gumster, J; Shimonski, Robert. 2010. *GIMP Bible*, Wiley Publishing, Inc.

Luke, Ali. 2012. *Publishing E-Book for Dummies*, John Wiley and Sons, Inc.

Web Sites

Here are some web sites that will provide you with information:

Amazon Kindle Direct Publishing
`https://kdp.amazon.com/`

Amazon Kindle Publishing Guidelines
`http://kindlegen.s3.amazonaws.com/AmazonKindlePublishin gGuidelines.pdf`

Barnes & Noble Bookstore `http://www.barnesandnoble.com`

Calibre `http://calibre-ebook.com`

Calibre Tips
`http://www.teleread.com/drm/the-abcs-of-format-conversion-for-the-kindle-sony-and-nook-plus-some-calibre-tips/`

E-Book Reader Matrix
http://wiki.mobileread.com/wiki/E-book_Reader_Matrix

GIMP http://www.gimp.org

HTML http://www.w3schools.com/html/

jEdit http://www.jedit.com

Kindle Previewer
http://www.amazon.com/gp/feature.html?docId=1000765261

Kindle Previewer User's Guide
http://kindlepreviewer.s3.amazonaws.com/UserGuide.pdf

Nook Press
https://www.nookpress.com/

Nook for PC
http://www.barnesandnoble.com/u/nook-for-pc/379003591/

Nook for Windows 8
http://www.barnesandnoble.com/u/nook-for-windows-8/379003757

Nook for Mac
http://www.barnesandnoble.com/u/nook-for-mac/379003592/

Sigil Editor http://code.google.com/p/sigil

TextPad http://www.textpad.com

Glossary

ASIN

Amazon Standard Identification Number. This ia a 10 digit number used to identify books published by Amazon.

CSS

Cascading Style Sheets

HTML

Hyper-Text Markup Language

JPEG

Joint Picture Experts Group. This is the most common digital image format. JPEG files have a .jpg extension.

KOLL

Kindle Owners Lending Library

ISBN

International Standard Book Number. This is a 10 or 13 (if assigned after 2007) digit number used to identify a book.